D1450827

Praise for *Lavando la Dirty Laundry*

This writer warns us she is a woman like a "Mexican electric fence." And yet between the sheets or between the murmur of the rolling pin, we are trusted to overhear confidences between intimates. It is on the white sheets of this book that a woman's most private confessions are transformed from dirty laundry to poetry luminescent as linen on the line. I truly feel gratitude for being allowed to read such private dialogues. It is a book that is a remove from other Texas writers in its capacity to encompass the globe, as Chicana poetry should in the new millennium. I feel very privileged to be allowed to give this book its blessing.

—Sandra Cisneros
author of *The House on Mango Street*, *Caramelo* & others
MacArthur Foundation Fellow

Soaked in the bubbling sizzle of *memorias herviendo*, these poems are everything but a stain rubbed clean. Sometimes the safest form of remembrance comes through the act of forgetting. But these are not safe poems. They do not have a safety net or a forewarning and they recall what some would rather forget. They are lessons in the comfort and healing that comes through sharing and telling. And tell they do. The poesia of the what-was, lying comfortably next to the poemas of the what-is. That is what makes them so alarming!

—Levi Romero
Author of *Sagrado: A Photopoetics Across the Chicano Homeland*
& *A Poetry of Remembrance: New and Rejected Works*

This exquisite collection of poems by Natalia Treviño enchants and exposes, drawing the reader into its center surely, passionately, and as fiercely as a wildfire. *Lavando La Dirty Laundry* is sensual and direct, and wraps its articulate fingers firmly around your heartstrings until the reader is carried off on a magical tour through continents, cultures, languages, and marital states. Reaching everything from motherhood to cancer, and love to the hand of God, Treviño leaves us with indelible images of life at its most valiant. A premier collection by a young poet who exhibits clearly a master's touch.

—Carmen Tafolla
author of *Sonnets and Salsa*, *Curandera*, & others
First Poet Laureate of San Antonio

More Praise for *Lavando la Dirty Laundry*

From legacies of last meals, laundries, lands and islands, and all along silver rivers where there *could have been thunder outside, /islands above our heads, splitting the sky* and surely sky splits and families tumble out fourteen lost babies and leave six surviving. Where the empanadas are sold at dawn, *four kilos each morning,/ for your daughters, /their dresses, for school, the right dresses.* Where someone must *wake at three and start kneading* as we need more nourishment before melanoma begins to peel away the organ of life once love is nourished in this, our, generation of living. And in Natalia Treviño's *Lavando la Dirty Laundry*, we finally come to understand how we *breathe, how hearts multiply/their rooms second by second/, how earth shifts to remind us/of new day, how air is enough/ to feed thousands of oceans and their pups.* And how if we had known this, known what Trevino brings, we *wouldn't have spent so much time ripping/ blades of grass between* (our) *teeth/ to see how black storms/ enter their leaves as green light.* And would have *thought only flora/could feed on wisps, lap the light.* Just as she guides us to know in this book of knowing. Treviño solidly delivers in her debut presentation, an admirable poetic; a knowing we all need, must read.

–Allison Adelle Hedge Coke,
author of *Burn, Blood Run, Off-Season City Pipe, & others*
American Book Award Winner

Throughout Natalia Treviño's sparklingly humorous, tenderly grim, and wise first collection, "dirty laundry" serves as a brilliant metaphor for a courageous, unblinking examination of interwoven cultures and generations. The poems of *Lavando La Dirty Laundry* give us the stories of wives, from *abuelas* and *tias* in Mexico, figures from Greek epics and the New Testament, as well as from the contemporary narrator who speaks of the sourness of a former marriage and the sweet nourishment of a new one that joins two cultures from opposite sides of the globe. Old, soiled laundry, in this collection, takes on new life, its cleaned threads glimmering with fresh breath in the intricate weavings of this must-read book.

—Wendy Barker
author of *Nothing Between Us: The Berkeley Years* & others
Poet-in-Residence, UT San Antonio

LAVANDO
LA DIRTY LAUNDRY

Norman, Oklahoma
2013

FIRST EDITION, 2014

Lavando La Dirty Laundry
© 2014 by Natalia Treviño

ISBN 978-0-9851337-5-7

Cover Image:
Hills Hoist Installation at Bondi Beach, Australia
© Andrew Baines 2013

Mongrel Empire Press
Norman, OK

Online catalogue: www.mongrelempire.org

Book Design: Mongrel Empire Press using iWork Pages

For Stewart and Stuart,
my guides and loves

And for Palmer Hall,
friend of this work

Acknowledgments

Inheritance of Light (University of North Texas Press): "Zapatos Blancos"

Borderlands: Texas Poetry Review: "Cooling Near the Center"

Octavo, The Poetry Quarterly for the Alsop Review: "Sacred Heart," "Mexican Bride," "Penelope Yes," "Bodies of Knowledge"

Voices de la Luna Online Poetry Journal: "Evening Apology," "It Was the Chef Who Finally Explained"

Houston Literary Review: "Música Caprichosa: For My Mother Who Wanted to Play," "The Function of Swelling in Pregnancy"

The Sugar House Review: "Tortilla Skins"

burntdistrict: "Graft Draft"

Sliver of Stone Magazine: "The Gyre Up Close and In the Kitchen," "Second Marriage, Stew," "After the Melanoma"

Gracias & Thank You

None of this work can be done alone. All of it is written in gratitude to the many voices who are beckoned and echoed on these pages, my family, my teachers, my beloveds. With the 'black squiggly lines' on *this* page, to borrow my dear Professor Mark Allen's favorite expression as we navigated Medieval Lit, I am grateful to have a glimpse into the enormity of it all. I am grateful to my poetry mother and mentor, Wendy Barker, for her patience with revisions, visions and revisions, for her hope, and for her incredible friendship. To Sandra Cisneros, I am especially grateful, for waking me up with the Alfredo Moral de Cisneros Award for Emerging Writers and for her generous wisdom and inspiration to remind me of the importance of *ganas* to take our hopes from childhood and make them realities.

To my dear friend and fellow *trampa*, Levi Romero, I owe many fields of gratitude for helping me believe I can do this, and without whom I would have never met Jeanetta Mish, my wise, brave, and patient publisher. I thank Levi for the final push to help this book find a home at Mongrel Empire Press when it was clear that its original publisher and my dear friend Palmer Hall at Pecan Grove Press would be unable to publish it before his passing in 2013.

For my dear willow-friend and guide, Allison Adelle Hedge Coke, who, with gentle tapping, helped catapult these poems to where they sit today. Many thanks to Carmen Tafolla, a most giving light here in the heart of San Antonio, for inspiring me and paving such a good way. Many thanks to Kacee Belcher, my former student who crept into my heart, stayed there for the long haul, became a writer in her own right, and gave me a clean editorial reading of the poems in this book. I also owe miles of thank you's to my dear friends and colleagues, Barbara Griest-Devora and Ignacio Magaloni who are in these poems, for their infinite patience with my questions and for their keen, perpetual sight, and especially to Barbara who helped down to the last day. To her husband, Alexander Devora for his keen photographic eye and friendship.

To my fellow sisters and brothers in the Macondo Writer's Workshop including Macarena Hernandez, Erasmo Guerra, Levi Romero, Anel Flores, Liliana Valenzuela, Denise Chavez, Luis Rodriguez, and Lucha Corpi, the poet Ai, and iréne lara silva who at one moment or another guided me, and together with many wonderful members in workshop, taught me to about translingual writing—and so much more. *Aqui vamos, y nos veamos pronto, con amor.* It is unthinkable to put into words how much my "firsters" at The University of Nebraska and Omaha have helped me over the years—the ultra talented Jen Lambert, the poet-of-scene-Stephanie Austin, our dear Bill James, who out-Joyces Joyce, and lookout Terence Kelley, my personal war correspondent, for their constance and laughter, for their wisdom and beauty, and for their perpetual consideration of my fiction and poetry. An immeasurable gracias to Fred Arroyo, my Nebraska mentor who so conscientiously helped me learn to see *living language,* who so profoundly shaped my understanding of the magic objects make when they coalesce with the world through a highly aware narrative lens, and who has given me so many generous hours of his amazingly valuable and thorough perspective.

Many thanks also to my early 90's core group called *group*, Amy Williams-Eddy, Leah Flores, Barbara Griest-Devora, and our brave leader Wendy Barker, who guided our awareness of words and the electricity meter in poetry. Many thanks also to Norma Cantu for her kind and enthusiastic support of these poems in their early days, as well as the wonderful people at the Dorothy Sargent Rosenberg Foundation, and the San Antonio Artists Foundation, for their generous prizes, not only to me, but also to so many other writers who need that financial assistance to find time to write in the light of day. I am indebted to them for their collective belief that my poems deserve merit, time, and space. My unbending gratitude Stewart Horne, my beautiful husband, who sustains me daily—and who has a great editorial eye, and to my amazingly talented son, Stuart Morris who attends readings, and has given critique since he could speak. Both of you are both my soul's stewards, my heart's teachers, and my eyes' scouts. Gracias a my dear family Greg and Eileen in London, for their perpetual love and listening, to my incredible family, Christopher, Shelley, Beth and Don Horne in Australia, who have opened chambers in my heart I never knew existed. Many thanks to my one and only brother, Javier Treviño and his wife Karen, always for their loving support of my creative endeavors.

How to thank my parents, Martha and Bolo Treviño, for their support when I choose the path of studying words in English to either "eke out a living" or fulfill an unimagined version of the American Dream. How do I thank them for their bravery in raising me and Javi so far from our birthplace to raise us with the privilege of being both lost and found in a bi-national experience? So far from their language, their friends and family, their whole world? How to thank God, *La Virgen*, the stars, and the elements who have shaped my visions and my being?

I would also like add a special thank you to Andrew Boobier, a most encouraging editor at *Octavo Poetry Journal*, who gave several of these poems wings when they were just babies—in England of all places! Also a warm, calm seaside thank you to Andrew Baines, Australian artist, for his generosity, creativity, and artistic vision that synchronized on so many levels with my poems.

And to you, dear reader. Thank you.

CONTENTS

LAVANDO
LA DIRTY LAUNDRY

Natalia Treviño

LAVANDO Y QUEMANDO

Zapatos Blancos

What is it about white
that made my grandmother tell me
es que me siento joven
con zapatos blancos.

Is it the way white is clean,
new, the way it looked
on t-shirts she washed
for my grandfather, bleached crisp
fresh by her young hands?

Or is it the way white satin felt
draping over her princess figure
rounding over her linen-smooth arms,
her wedding day, summer, 1932?

Do white shoes remind her
of the day her mother made her rub
white *zapatitos*, until they sparkled,
until each small finger reddened at the fight?

Abuelita, do you feel suspended
on these memories when you walk
on white shoes? Is it that white
came first, Abuelita?

before your marriage promise,
before his t-shirts soiled,
before an egg was cracked?

Mexican Bride

Centered above her king-sized bed
in Nuevo Leon, a large crucifix, a resin-bloodied
crumpling Body of Christ—the only art
hanging from her smooth plaster walls.

A lamination of Mary, Mother of Sorrows tucked
across and below the frame of her vanity. Wedding
gifts for all new brides, decorations surrounding the spirit
in the bedroom. As if the dimensions of the body

nailed at the limbs would lead new husbands
to handle the living curves of their brides.
As if a slain nude, thorned at the crown above her
head, could help rigid legs relax, for fire.

The Happy Couple

He would spark a joint in the living room
Ask, "Wanna hit?"

He always said he wanted to be good to her.
Share his life. Stuff like that.

And Her Weaving

There could have been thunder outside,
islands above our heads, splitting the sky
during our last meal together. I cannot remember.

Or were the islands inside us somehow?
Already working their way into you,
glowing green, and silver rivers — maybe —

A landscape, tall mountains, folding,
purple cloth draped on holy ground.
Who am I to forget these things?

What calls you? Oils, battle–heaves, Odysseus?
I may never know this point in you,
where you gasp before another man's face,

gleam–streaked in blood. I should have
listened better that night, noticed if your arm
grazed mine in sleep —

What were the strings weaving?

It's the islands in my head
that weep the most; their skies
and rain, agape.

My O.

An Ex Recounts

How I wanted your friends outside our tent
to hear us, I breathed out loud, what it took.

Camping before had been only us and giving it over to the land.
With only stars, forest, horseflies to hear.

But you brought your friends on our next trip,
With them, you'd drink yourself drunk,

howl–laughing late, smoking pot
by heightened fire.

That night I washed our meal's dishes, by flashlight.
Grease slow to move in ice water. I went to bed alone.

So when you crawled into the tent, I started with a hand.
Wanted to put out your forgetting me in the cold,

And when I took you in this way, ex,
I just needed someone to think,

even an audience of drunks,
that I could breathe.

Ulysses Thinks to Explain It

The woman-thing tore back from me:
her anemone touch left our pools of wet to stick

under my leg. Crying, she said, her eyes,
wide with the sight. Your wife is crying, always, Ulysses.

She turned me away, film of her cloak, ballooned.
Even before the first battle, there'd already been rivers—

You know that, Wife. Every day, tears, streaming over your face—
afraid I would leave you, breath-failed, wide-browed.

Your stomach large from the baby. Could have been a double
headed witch who told you things, lies about me, a sorceress

splitting your mind. It was the ocean I could taste,
Woman; wanting no salt from tears in my breath.

Kill and know it was my hand sending in the sword.
With you, silence murdered with no blood.

No echo—I could still love you, Wife. I could soak your dresses,
spin you a fleet, though you work on your strings,

your hands covered in lines, threads crossing one another,
weaving eyes into animals and the goddesses. Save you, you say.

You always weave eyes so big on their faces,
unattractive in women.

Penelope Yes

she remembered his ring hovering
over her

his lapis on gold
while their skins moved

between it she unravels
all night whispered her maids

shunned the practice
they'd seen watched

her once covered in threads
eyes closed her whole body in a stream

of colors thighs
in purple arms golden red

fingers lost
among the crossings

of legs arms
so many lines

New Window

Leaving for once, Aphrodite decided
the grounds needed investigating.
At night, Buttercups waxed open.

She knew never let man or god
block her view of the fields, but her Adonis fled
past them, past her heaviness too —

worked his spear into the gut of a hunt instead.
She'd forgotten how grasses once soaked in her hair,
how trees folded under her step.

She only need remember the syntax of sky,
voweling hunger of the clouds,
the clenching of roots for molten earth.

For ages, she wanted to contain him
in the cusp of her belly, and worked
her way around his boredom, offering popping berries,

the juice inside dripping apples, revealing the bottom
of her earthly ache. His gaze, she decided, would stay
a gaze, wide, dreaming of four legs crumbling.

He would rather
sleep. Than wake.

Fish and Hunt, Hunger

Adonis didn't need to sleep
with Aphrodite. Close to the banks
of the underworld, he would head
out early for fish and game.

When she emerged from the stream,
hips so rounded—magnolia-mouthed—
wearing cloth so clear, his line
to the catch unraveled.

She watched his grip,
how his foot seeped into mud.
Some other large beast might miss
his practiced lure.

And once after, when she lifted herself
from him, the horizon disappeared
behind her blank skin, curving,
and she gave him a strand of hair.

For fishing, she said, *for luck*.
And she tied it to his line, knowing
it would shimmer and creatures, all of them
would come to him. Hungry.

Tía Licha

You lost
fourteen babies, kept six.
Held us at the cheeks, grandmother's sister,
Tía Licha, landing kiss after kiss — sucking warm pockets
through wrinkled lips right at our ears near our noses.

You told me
how you sold empanadas at dawn
four kilos each morning, for your daughters,
their dresses, for school, the right dresses.
Wake at three and start kneading

the dough,
boiling *la piña, el camote, y la leche*
or filling ninety-six pastries each
morning. Seven breakfasts too,
and not one bite for you. On the sidewalk

selling every morning.
Your husband sold you
the flour, fruit, and milk from his store,
kept track of his inventory. Kept you quiet
and pregnant each year you were married.

You took care
of Santita, your neighbor, someone's *tía abuela*,
too sick, too old to cook, a lady
just a few blocks away, just a few hundred meters.
So hungry too, needed toast and coffee, her juice, *un huevito*

every morning,
and *su platito* for lunch. La *comida*. And, and, and
it was nothing, you say—
    pero con la sopa, su aguacate, su tortilla bien caliente,
    el pollo deshebrado—all of it by the old lady's noon.
How you'd walk fast around the corners,
never spill a drop of *la sopita, el fideo, el caldito.*

Told me
you were seventy when you learned
women had *los orgasmos*. Read this
from the book, a medical book about women.
Said up to then, you thought sex was nothing but a violation.

You lean
into my son's face, great great aunt, *tía abuela*,
close your eyes as you kiss him and all the children,
the widow's bump behind your neck,
curved like half a globe on your back.

Before the Divorce

The belly had soured so often.
She thought it her natural propensity.

Something inherited, her mother's
Inability to digest.

LOS NIÑOS AND OTHER QUEHACERES

Translating Birth

My grandmother once told me,
todos mis partos fueron bonitos
of her five births. In Spanish,
the word for birth is *parto*,
and being raised gringa,
I had been translating words to English

by removing the *o*. It almost always worked:
banco, bank, santo, saint. And with *a*, I also had success:
computadora, ador-a. Adore. *Flor-a*.
But not all words fit this rule. There was no *birtho*,
and Bertha was a name, not a cognate:
a-bierto and *a-bierta* did not work—to open is not to be born.

The Spanish for born was *nacer*. There was no *nace*.
At least birth and born alliterated in Texas.
Nacer and *parto* did not. I heard *all of my partings were pretty.*
Could the language be that wise?
The child parts. Departs? *Departe de* meant *from whom*.
I saw the baby as a part that came from the mother.

I could see the opposite of what she said, the ugly partings.
Cuts. Splits. *Parte la carne. Se partió por en medio.*
Cut the meat. It split itself down the middle.
Me parto el corazón por mis hijos, tío Jorge said.
And on an operating table, he did split his heart for his children.

I ask this of a language where
the heads of pigs hang above sodas
three houses away. Where newspapers print, *¡Accidente!*
above bright photos of half-bodies, twisted, red metal.
Where with this same paper,
they wrap the meat you will eat for lunch.

Standard Loss Couplets

Breasts too large still, after the miscarriage,
And the belly still protrudes.

The plate holding spoiled food
Must still be washed, dried, stacked.

The Function of Swelling in Pregnancy

1.

Fortunately, the swelling that comes with pregnancy
does go down. Watery ponds in wrists,
moveable lakes in ankles,
waters damned behind the stretch

of translucent skin. *Water,*
the doctors say, *you're retaining*
so much. Drink more, they say.
You're lookin' puffy.

And pregnant women eye the mirror
for signs of skin not puffed. Left
eyelid maybe, top of this knuckle.
But there are bigger problems: standing,

not being able to stand,
the ache for sitting.
Unwashed dishes that pile
in the deepening sink.

2.

When the babies are born, new mothers
check floating uterus under skin.
A wet chamois. Feel the dough to knead.
The uterus is tilted the doctors say.

May not pee on your own;
squeeze your nipples like this. The sitz, yes —
that. He's not latching on, dehydrate
if you don't make him eat every two

hours. Wake him up, undress him. Have to
piss him off. Cleft chin! You know,
That's a birth defect. Yes, the mother-law says —
I will smoke in front of the baby.

During the birth, levied thick wrists have burst rivers,
legs, bottoms, and eyes flooded the room.
Mother and child, all moist air now, all in the quiet
fog behind a steady rush of the waterfall they formed,
of flesh
and blood
and milk.

The Mother Who Tried

Before bed, my son told me, You're not you anymore.
You're like my shoes. When they're tied too tight!

I'd been reading discipline books,
experts' rules for four-year-olds, and he spoke his first poem.

Well, God

for my grandmother and my aunt, Raquenel y Raque

1980

In your orange, plastered room,
Abuelita, by your chair near the open
Door, the paint had split, the wall brown

In places where humid wires bled wetness into walls,
Cracked in the heat. When you die,
I asked you, who will take care of Raque?

At ten, I knew grandparents died—and Raque,
I knew was not right. Angled teeth.
Down's-happy smile. Mind, they said, of a two-year-old.

Though she was over thirty. Laughed at my navel. *Hoyito?*
Hoyito, she'd sing, poking, pinching pretend holes
In my belly—squinting. Looked Chinese, though she was not.

My little girl shoes fit her soft, bent feet.
My forgotten dolls became her new babies.
Oi, oi, oi, she'd coo them and play

While we talked the serious talk in the next room.
I worried about logistics. We lived in the States.
You, Abuelita, across the border. I had a life. I was in fifth grade.

And there was cooking to do. I knew that. I knew
People needed money. They had to count. Reading was necessary
Even in Mexico. Cars run people over when they don't look.

What I learned in second grade I tried to teach her.
Numbers. *Uno. Dos.* How letters made the sounds our favorite
Clown sang when we watched his show on the blurry tv.

I wanted her to sing with me, *¡Que sal-ga Pi-po!*
To make the bed. She laughed, offered me a doll.
Pinched its belly. Pointed to my new shoes, and said, *Mios?*

1945
How you wanted a daughter, Abuelita,
In your life of two maids, a drinking husband,
And darling-tough boys: you had wanted a soft girl,

In cotton. She'd spoon eggs into flour,
Spread masa into the folds of dry husks—
She'd know when steam compotes the fruit,

How meats could season into gifts for the mouth.
And, at night, while men drank, or went away,
you and your daughter would whisper near a window

Where la Silla de la Sierra silhouetted the sky.
But you had a third son instead, who died.
You swaddled him for the photo in his satin-baby box,

And you went looking for a daughter—
Outside, on the pavement, a beggar woman there
Giving away two children: a boy and a girl.

I will take your girl, you said.
And Raque was yours, Raquenel.
A girl you named after yourself.

Her black, shimmery hair, skin, clean as the new milk
Streaming from the birth-death of your son.
Your three brothers said no. They knew

Raque was not right. They were doctors.
Something about alcohol, the street, the mother—
Said take her back. *¡Dejala!*

When I was six I asked why she was like that.
You told me you already loved her
When you found out. In the hot light of your room,

Abuelita, I asked what everyone feared.
Who will take care of Raque when you die?
Pues, Diosito, you said without a pause.

And I heard all the combinations of your answer:
Well, God, Then, God, Well, Little God.
Three answers. One sentence.

We hardly felt
The heat's hold of the air.
You knew how few fans were needed.

How with some doors open,
You could keep
From over-heating.

Evening Apology

for my son, Stuart

What you hope is
not to miss some last glimpse

of this reeling, firefly night.
You've cast your body, rebellious,

the way a swordfish fights a man
on the other side of the sea.

You search, sometimes bleating,
for that nestling spot, your memory.

Who was I to replace my womb
with this cold, crumpled mattress?

The night you were born, you let me
know—out here is maybe not a good idea—

Breasts too large for your mouth,
gouging lights, fluorescent.

Bright fires in your belly
made you scream.

But we have moments, rapt silence,
of God saying,

this is the only
place I can put you for now.

Música Caprichosa
For my Grandmother who wanted to play

Summer 1931, you stood by the door 'Uelita,
only eleven, beads of sweat under your tight black curls

You hid behind the door
had run to your first lesson in piano, your heels

pressed to the threshold. The aunt, *esa tía,*
the mean one, a step, not blood, was your teacher

and you could hear her sister from the other side of the door:
To that one? *Le vas a dar classes a esa largona?*

To that dummy?
What for?

You turned and ran home, crushing dirt clumps
beneath your shoes, the black patent dulled in the dust.

You never touched
a piano, or a music lesson after that.

They never asked you or your mother
where you went. Why you missed.

Ramiro could sing. Your older, handsome brother.
Operas, they thought. And the aunts and the teachers

came. Free lessons for his voice,
His rounded notes. Took photos for his trip,

¡Para irse a Hollywood¡ Ese Ramiro! ¡Tan guapo!
And then tissue that should not grow behind his brain.

And there was no money. You tell me your mother climbed
the steps *del palacio* to beg the governor, her gold-gray

hair pulled back tight, for respect.
Dressed in her long black skirt, like *buena gente.*

Had never begged in her life. Made that clear,
but he can sing, *por favor;*

She trembled.
Es mi hijo.

And the governor sent his own doctor,
paid for the boy who could sing

for free surgeries, books, and more lessons
for his voice. You say Ramiro

knew what day he would die —
had read there would be blue fingers

in the books a doctor gave him. And he called out
from his bed, *Ya estan negras*, Mama! Black!

Days before, he'd chased you down the bus routes
in cold rain.

You had been sneaking bus rides
to see your secret boyfriend, *Buelito*.

Ramiro was right. That was the day
it happened, the day fingers turned black.

*

Now, 'Uelita, in your translucent sleep,
you pee sometimes, sing, or dream.

Your little sister wakes you with a song
and I see your face again as you whisper

in tune with her. You keep
Ramiro's photo for Hollywood hanging

on your melon-painted wall,
a head shot.

Mother to Child

After a meal, we lie down for sleep.
My five-year-old son presses his ear
to my belly, hears the commotion

undulating—the glass of wine,
bits of spinach and wild rice, bite of chocolate truffle.
I lean in with my ear toward his flat center.

I hear the canals run inside him.
The sloshing of a harbor, at night.
A moon pulling the splashes close.

He returns to my puffed stomach,
asks, Are you doing that on purpose?
Are you making those sounds?

No, I say. Now he's confused.
It sounds like the bubbles fish hear.
Maybe a boat, I answer.

I tell him we have the same sounds
inside us. His eyes widen.
He presses his ear again and he sees

engines forming under our skins,
churning our salty waters
in unison. Our first tide.

Observable Rules

I tell my son it is not polite to open other people's refrigerators
—and never touch their stove. At home, white doors fly open;
he lingers in bright light facing transparent shelves
lined with red bottles, grained mustards, and piled brown eggs.

Maybe that is why men stand clear of the kitchen
—out of politeness. Learned to leave private shelves alone.
Avoiding ovens that burn, surfaces that smolder.
Following an observable rule from childhood.

Keep the doors shut—the way Mom said.

The counselor said love is like millions of atoms trying
to re-combine, pulled in by gravity, or some strong force.
I try to dream of love, and it comes as milk, as white puddle,
the first rule we learn.

What could be easier to swallow?

SECRETOS DE LA COCINA

Lavando la Dirty Laundry

'Uelita, we were kneading the flour on your metal kitchen table
when you told me my grandfather had girlfriends.

Measuring granules of salt. You said it explained the day
he threw your ironing into the mud.

There you were, holding the steaming
iron in your hot cement house.

You heard a fellow at the front door, calling for my grandfather
Raul! Raul! Raul? And you let the man in,

seated him in your home,
offered him agua fresca, for the heat.

'Uelito arrives in that moment.
Sees you handing

the fellow a drink,
screams, *¡Lárgate de aquí!*

Get Out!

Get Out!
¡Hijo de su madre! ¡Cabron!

Throwing the man and your fresh, hot whites
into the muddy street.

And he did not speak
to you for days. Left you to guess

what the fellow had done.
Your pile of laundry

flung to a trampled mess.
You gathered it,

left it sagging, soaking in a bucket
for days while the rain kept you from washing again.

Years later, after 'Uelito died,
the fellow came again:

He thought you were cheating with me, he said.
I'd seen him with a girl.

And he thought you and I were
like them.

You tell me this and press the dough into the tin
clang of the table, a metal heart yielding below your fingers.

Tortilla Skins

In the hot light of your kitchen, 'Uelita, you show me how to press the thick dough against your popping, aluminum table. Your hands the size of the tortillas to come, willing the mass to open as a soft disk. My hands too small to maneuver, to stretch over it, to pull the dry powder in. I was fifteen and knew you were happy. Years after 'Buelito had died, you were a new kind of woman. Certain eyes. Laughing, traveling, playing cards. Able to wake and say no, to skip the simmering heat of *guisados* and flame-burnt *tortillas* by the main noon meal. Bake a cake instead, at night. Crochet and smoke at the same time. Speak up around the men. Accept a small glass of beer. The dough as cool as your hands, your red fingernails disappear into the ball. Would you remarry? I ask. You are quick to answer. Yes, it is ugly to live alone. Your fingers have memorized this motion, the bend of this mass. All I can think is how wives in Mexico flail in sick waters, in tired, wakeful oceans, choppy white crests salting their faces, silenced and gasping by the slap of spray. Romantic novella endings are kneaded into the eyes and ears of their daughters, spiteful neighborhood *chisme*, the sealing orders from men, sons, brothers, husbands. The time folds on your face, 'Uelita, the veins rise on the back of your hands. Portraits in your living room, bridal framed faces, faint as shells at the end of a flat beach, stripped of color by the brine of dry sunlight, waiting for the tide to soak them, turn them, or swallow them. Bone pushing out the skin at the back of your neck, you bend to your yes it is ugly to live alone. And we press our tortilla skins to the heat, their faces down, to cook.

The Gyre Up Close and In the Kitchen

Thank you, William Butler

In a room that is spinning,
One must have a table.

Though dishes may slide
To shatter,

Fly and slice,
Draw blood,

At least they had one
Moment, whole,

Near napkin, glass,
An eye.

It Was the Chef Who Finally Explained

How to make a good sauce.
You can't throw everything in together, he said.

You wait. First you let the onions cook
for a while in their own oil.

And you listen for them to crackle.
Only then, press the clove of garlic you will need.

Stir. They'll take each other in—
the two layers.

Create their own new liquid.
That is when you add tomato, or whatever you want.

You wait each time you add a spice.
Building one new flavor one at a time.

They'll embed themselves if you do this.
Like a good marriage—

Each one will hold the other
all the way down the throat.

A Lesson of Elements

Mr. Howe the chemistry teacher told us we would make real soap when we were sixteen. It seemed unlikely and impossible and too liquidy, but we had his lesson plan. We had the elements. With a white chalky formula smattered on the board, the poster of the periodic table, the very elements themselves gleaming on the desk, counting on our quiz-tested heads, we knew the best secret of all, why molecules liked one another, how they always struggled to bond where there was the right opening. Wanting that fit. Dizzy steamy electrons inside atoms, fighting, spluttering, pushing, and pulling each other like woozy solar systems drowning in each other's micro-fluxy juices. So when we put the green balls of waxy liquid-solid that did not smell so great into the water, our hands they came out clean and soapy, just like Mr. Howe said they would, and the gritty, dirty microbes must have been very happy, bonded inside all those open mouths, those sweet, watery nooks that pulled them in, each grainy, dirty molecule nested inside its own wet swirl, married forever down that drain in that bubble pop of destiny.

Cooling, Near the Center

After the divorce, the refrigerator became my favorite
place to shelve. Capers, olives, long after they had been opened.
Chocolates next to onions. Spinach aging in a twisted bag.

Beveled bottles and their heart-strung names, *Alessi, Hill Country,*
Cold Pressed and Organic. I'd started with this appliance new.
Slowly, it began to fill. Asparagus, pine nuts, edible flowers.

But grape tomatoes wrinkled in their piles.
The golden soup, in the cold, divided. Whitened.
The rosemary loaf from the restaurant, turned, caked-over—

Lost compositions in that thing. Staring into the whiteness,
I'd never find Holy in here. Solids, warm flavors, flesh—
ingredients survive only so long in cold.

On a stove, they could come together.

Enriched Wife

I was not trained to cook by my mother.
She sent me far from the kitchen,
from slicings, vapors, flames.

This wasn't a practical way to raise a Mexican girl.
My Texan neighbors made iced tea,
practiced their boiling with soft white pouches

that would steep. Thawed ground meat
with electric skillets after school.
Handled knives with soapy water,

skinned, chopped, and boiled potatoes. As a new
wife, my cooking never went well.
I could only go so far remembering what you do in a kitchen.

Reading ingredients, cookbooks, the backs of cans
and boxes, guessing at the meaning of the lexicon:
pre-heat, blend, mix, sear, braise.

Knowing the words is not enough
to make rice, or any good dish.
Years later I learned white rice had no use,

no nutrition. Bleached of its brown
vitamins. Enriched later in a machine.
Yet it was the only good rice I knew.

In Mexico, I asked my grandmother and her sister
for directions how to make their rice
so fluffed, so golden and red.

You always start with a little oil, *mi'ja*
and a high flame; add the diced onions
and cook until they glaze like pearls.

That is when you add the rice, my aunt says.
Let it sizzle. *Hasta que se pone casi transparente.*
Stir in a crush of garlic, a bit of salt.

Then, boiling broth, *mi'ja.*
It must be boiling, *de pollo*, they agreed.
or the rice will break, they both said.

I do this with brown rice now,
olive oil, a veggie broth,
tomatoes, and warmed pumpkin seeds.
Enriched Mexican rice.

AMOR SAGRADO:
DESDE MELANOMA HASTA MAGDALENA

Drug Store

Suddenly, boyfriend, I could feel your absence at the counter—
the prescription in my hands.

An infection raged
in my throat, and we were still practically strangers.

When buying groceries with the ex,
he'd disappear, go off to other aisles.

I shopped alone though he was somewhere in the store.
And now you did the same thing—men.

I wondered which aisle had your attention.
Fishing magazines? Donuts?

How many rows I would walk
before I found you. I didn't know how

the mother cardinal waits—
her mate gone. How he returns, a feeding

folded in his beak.
I was done.

And I found you an aisle away,
shopping for my lozenges.

In the Direction of Words

When I married you, I knew what to make of vows, how they spin and vanish. Even sloshing caps in rivers disappear midsummer. So many droughts, limestone promises, ravines broken by dust. Earthly vows said and unsaid, said and un-felt, un-done, (we'd both undone them once already) but you kept reminding me of Beowulf, how it can be that a smart-souled man knows that words must match works, how the scythe whispering by the tuft of flowers told Frost we can work together even when we are apart. How our words could maybe get into an apartment together, furnished, folkloric, indigenous, open-hearted constellations flickering on our ceiling, melon-papaya-chayote colored walls, avocado trees blooming amidst gum tree shaving cream and San Antonio River-front eyeliner. Rain-forest, fire-proof saltshakers and teacups next to steaming tortilla puffed meat pies (oh and the opal-corn-steamed bed sheets we could make), buttered and feathered like the tropical black of flying wings, red and green as the blue mountains themselves. Whispering into our hollow-airborn-pillows that stream along cloudlessness between the blue-green seasons that merge above the oceans—and when I vowed to you—this second time I vowed—I breathed to God that I will stay with the man standing next to me because the highway I bridged together between my words and what I did, between the words that once whirred invisible like an overheated mirage and their matching cowboy boots became the arc that carries me weightless to the shore.

Wedding Dress

Is it okay if I wear a raspberry-
reddish color for the wedding? I ask.
I won't wear white again.

I stopped loving red somewhere,
or I've forgotten it. I became off-
white sometime before we met,

or sand, hints of almost beige.
I'd filled my closet with creams, oatmeals,
Colors like a clean floor. Neutral carpets.

I looked good in mute.
Even my shoes disappeared.
Cream leggings. Eggshell flats.

I tried all the dresses they made
for second brides. Older women. Hazy blues.
Misted florals. Wistful, muted scallops.

And my mother held up a dress
I'd chosen for her,
A strapless raspberry.

Latticed above the knee.
Why not this she said.
We laughed.

Wet roses, cinnamon.
I could do this.
Wear incense.

Heading Home Without Mr. Sky

Firm, he asked, do you like the mattress firm?
And well there was only one response to that.

Firm is good in bed, especially when the stars
Are ordering things around.

Having traveled from planet to planet, she had
seen how big the rings of Saturn really were,

and Jupiter's spot knew of her aching all too well.
Mr. Sky, though, had the trick in his bag—gave her a candle

to peek at herself in the mirror. Said candles
like that come our way once, maybe twice a lifetime.

So she packed his mattress and candle into her skin
And decided to wear nothing for a while,

until her eyes could adjust.

To The Husband Who Does Love Me

When you asked, I whispered yes I'd marry you,
so my heart could not hear.
It was deaf anyway.

No more could harm it,
even in a marriage.
But it could read lips.

Poisoned, it lagged and bled on the sidewalk.
Sheared, it grafted onto other organs—
I'd guess at directions,

foil shadows
that threatened darkness,
rely on eyes, ears, skin.

Second Marriage, Stew

for my husband, Stewart

With what ingredients I happen to have—
small chicken thigh, chayote squash, carrot,

red and blue potato. I am cooking for you while you lie sick.
Have been, long before we met, you say.

Marry me you asked in Australia.
We'd been walking miles by the beach

that morning on Shortland Esplanade
You say I took ten minutes to answer.

But we moved your salt and pepper shakers
across the planet, old records, your antique mugs.

The visa gave you twelve weeks to marry me.
It is week four, and you sweat in bed with the flu.

You left a hot summer in December.
Arrived a day later to wet winter.

Our shots are always a year behind yours,
you tell me. The flu takes its time

to travel the earth's continents.
Caught us both by surprise.

Cutting the squash through
blemished green skin, I see

a slim disk in the center has begun to turn.
A sudden red smoothness, a red lip near the stem

centered in the vapid pale green. Still chilled
and somewhat respectable, it opens firm, dices clean.

How would this squash taste,
having waited so long, stored in cold?

Your fever a raging stew, mid-boil,
We could go out for dinner, you say, reaching from the bed.

And this poem surfaces from the reddening,
ready for my lips.

The Wife Learns of Australian Demographics

You dream of red dust storms off the Australian coast.
Remember green skies meant hail. In summer,
roads screeched aflame, cars too slow for the wildfire winds,
how people boiled alive in their own bath tubs.

I read it's men in dark cloaks,
(not the Boogie man) that children fear in Australia—
men from the church
who rob Aboriginal babies from their mother's arms.

You explained the church men
wanted to help them, cleanse the living squalor,
heal the unclean. And now the brown children,
Stolen, cry for apology.

And you think of your own sister
a White child, born to unwed parents.
They only saw a swaddled pink circle,
the top of her head, as the nuns took her so far.

Shock

You are my husband,
yet you love me.

My serrated, magnetic teeth.
My one volt eye.

This second marriage
is converting my circuitry.

Reversing the current
in my angry blood.

No one should try to climb this
Mexican electric fence.

Don't you know about the shards of glass
that dried into my concrete walls?

Reach over, and you will bleed.
Who would want a woman like that?

But I collapse into your hands like snow.
My edges grounded between your fingers.

There Was a Girl Named Happy

You say you knew her when you saw her.
Dreamt about her when you were fourteen.
Missed her the first time around.

You are dedicated to her gardens now,
grow lavender because she likes the scent,
but her tears slash you.

I told you she was a myth.
But you lit candles for her anyway
and you gave me her ring.

How The Inner Peace Treaty Began

The yoga teacher said the breath,
the mind and the body were one
and so when the breath said
it would try anyway
the body was glad—
but the mind kept staring.

Foreign Coin

We fly apart in the summer:
both far south, both to the sea,
a hemisphere apart, me to Mexico, you to Australia,
the line between us as wide as my body braced to yours —
a Pacific stretch, our backs arched
like a bow, your torso long, and your fingers reach both coasts,
my open chest burns in the day, during your night.

Our planes return the same night, almost in unison:
our luggage bursting, tagged "Heavy."
We pile our gifts on the bed,
a miniature Spanish Galleon, *pintado a mano*,
a bag of cheese Twisties and Burger Rings.
Translucent opals threaded by gold,
a silver frog de Talpa — with two human front teeth.

A Christmas package from your son.
Lambs' wool insoles from your daughter,
large tins of Australian Breakfast Tea.
A Rugby League jersey.
Poker chips from tío Mayco's trip to Vegas.
A Catrina mermaid figurine, her black,
braided hair splashed against exposed bones.

That night under the blankets,
we reach for each other, your jet lag excised,
my forgiving exhaustion, but you make my leg flex.

My foot reaches to the edge of the bed —
touches something cold, a coin dropped from your jeans.
I finger the relief in my hand and see the face:
The Queen of the Commonwealth.

I reach to put it with the rest of our change.
You take it from my hand. Swirl it
in with the coins from my trip. I like mixing
my coins with yours, you say. Aztec glyphs
surround the Aboriginal elder. Feeding eagles
land on the Queen's silver cheek.
In your hands, I can hardly tell them apart.

Waking Up With Mr. Sky

If I had known you,
how you like to seep into floors
between rafters, wires, ceilings,
how you like the echo in my lungs,
how your dust glistens in the sunlight
that I breathe, how hearts multiply
their rooms second by second,
how earth shifts to remind us
of new day, how air is enough
to feed thousands of oceans and their pups.
If I had known you, I
wouldn't have spent so much time ripping
blades of grass between my teeth
to see how black storms
enter their leaves as green light.
Had thought only flora
could feed on wisps, lap the light.
Did not know I could carry you, as well.

Cancer

Two boys get out of a car in traffic. The car leaves
them carrying a loaded basket of laundry. A laundromat sits
across the street behind the Whataburger, the gas station.

The older one helps the younger balance as the basket tips.
Sheets, jeans, and towels stacked high above the rim between
them, the only people walking on this street.

Honey, your age never frightened me.
I'm no spring chicken and you, fourteen years older.
At fifty, we all have to have something—

Blood pressure. Cholesterol.
But your seasons turned upside down
when you came to marry me from Down Under.

January isn't summer in Texas.
Would have been a winter day in June
when you saw it on your arm.

The oncologist said this type came on recently.
It was time in the Texas sun. Not forgetting
sunblock in childhood. Not that hole in the Australian ozone.

We look odd, I know, stepping on this street.
This long walk ahead of us.
This basket we carry.

The Texas Chute

At the beach we let waves crash over our heads.
Spindling our son between our wrists.
I haven't played in the ocean since childhood.
Hadn't felt its break loosen the grip of my legs.
I won't take him in without you—
my grip slippery in these waters.
The ocean swallow him into Eternity.

We take our child to the water park.
Gorge ourselves on The Six Chuter, Tornado,
and White Water Canyon. Speed into pools
of chlorine. Spread the SPF every few
hours. You wear the baseball hat, the sunglasses,
the sun-proof shirt. We slather more on you—
your reddening neck, your golden arms.

We're sure the Texas sun isn't hotter than Australia's,
always joked about your English skin,
but it came in a mole that burst. Would not heal.
A note from the doctor:
"Seventy five percent survival at stage one."
He circled stage 4. We did not catch it early.
Melanomas are tricky, he says. *Like to travel to the heart.*

It is our first appointment at the Cancer Research Center.
The oncologist is on the other side of the door.
The coffee is brewing for Tuesday's patients.

The light between us dim as shark skin.
We do not bring the children to these waters.
Our eyes cannot meet. If they do,
there will be oceans crashing through our heads.

After the Melanoma

They take small patches of skin
like cornflakes from your forehead.
They leave scalpeled wounds to drain out the sun.

A folded note is mailed to us a week later.
Early cancer treated is stamped inside, askew.
Next appointment: six months.

The Texas sun might have burned you this way.
But some say it is your first forty-eight years
in Australia, where the ozone is thin.

Woven sarapes cover the heads of women
in Mexico. They walk with hands open,

their babies bundled in spiral of cloth
across their chests.

Daughters' heads are covered like living Catholic
idols. Their dark eyes look out from a pointed, woolen tent,

yellow, pink, and thin, faded orange.
Their skin is browning through the peak of fabric.

A folded note of warning.

Graft Draft

I have to say that your organ that keeps you together is becoming a disappointment. It wants to give in to the sun too much, so thin and pink. Ready for more melanomas. They take you, sure, every three months to check it, and yes they cut off the bad pieces, some benign, some not, and of course new skin comes back, but I am reminded you see—that this is just a short time we get together, at least in these skins, so we have to figure out a way to keep it going if one of us has to leave you know, seeya—if something really bad happens here in this realm of our palms. I propose something maybe it is crazy but you can think about it— I mean you are in no immediate danger that I can see, except for the headaches. They did tell us melanomas like to go to the brain but I try not to think about that—and your lymph surgery did go well so I have nothing to complain about, but I think maybe if I take my brown skin off for you and give it to you, I would be okay with that—at least while you headed to the store or something which they said can be dangerous to your skin because last time the dermatologist did say were you wearing your sunscreen, and I know you do but that time we went shopping you didn't and I could see the sun burning your forehead while we were walking to the car. I was hoping to give you some of my brown skin you see so we wouldn't have to worry so much. There are a lot of freckles and moles and spots you have and I can't tell them apart, so when the dermatologist told me to sit down at your last check up, I took it to mean he did not care if I could spot a bad one—I am sure this is not the case but I would have liked a little lesson right there with the right light and his eyes teaching mine to look at your skin a bit more like an expert like he does. I can joke I am an expert of your skin but we both know we have no idea what is keeping your skin together or tearing it apart, so why not just let's switch from time to time or let me do the extra errands outside and you don't leave the house without my skin okay because really if I am wearing your skin it may sag and all since you are bigger than me but I can deal with that since I am just wanting to be in your skin anyway—wink wink. It is warm and I always like it all over me—this would just make it sweeter between us and saltier too because I do sweat more than you— you know that and we would never fight over whose skin is whose and I would be good at taking care of your skin if you would let me and let mine soak up the sun it is already used to I think for generations, getting ready for something like this. I can't think what else it is good for.

Sacred Heart

Mary Magdalene
wasn't a prostitute. But it helped explain her

hundreds of years after she lived.
Named scarlet, hidden under desert sands.

Gospel secrets
that she'd been loved best, by Christ—

that she'd calmed apostles,
and best knew his heart.

How drops
of his blood

cooled in the folds
of her hand.

But what is it inside the heart
of a man? a god? or a law?

In medical books that explain the heart,
pages show how blockages persist.

Women kept from vestments
because Christ only chose men.

Entire lifetimes halted by the tartar
of human veins.

And without emphasis, passion, or gore,
passages tell of the unseen:

how a pale gold liquid,
camouflaged by all the red,

soothes spent cells,
nourishing the darkest vessels

Mary's mouth-kisses buried
in the deserts:

her secret sediments
in perpetual resurrection.

Mary Magdalene Sings

Though It Is Wrong For Me To Say

Jesus, my love, you didn't have to do it
that way, accept the thrush. Wings, flutter
of beatings, serrated beaks against your back.
We'd only but touched in good ways —
And wife of yours I was.
But you, also the wife of God —

His scout father blood coursing
in shadows under my dress,
his sallow linens, bellows with your sweat.
His carved spoon brined by the blood
from your bones. His bread soaked
in the plot to split your wrists.

You said even my mother could rise.
Enter his kingdom. We'd never thought of kingdoms —
knew their slaves who'd flee, and die,
their hollow eyes. You say murderers,
even the forked hats that would hammer
bars into your ankles, all can enter the kingdom.

Husband, that night, blankets
I wanted to give you. Your body open
to the rain. My face — ready for pluck
and the ants gathered at my feet as you died.
Hundreds upon me before I knew, crawling
curled like frightened dirt to my feet and legs.

At home that night, your mother fed the children,
saw my bitten feet and mixed a mud,
cool black blood from the earth,
swept it over the angry skin until I slept,
this water and blood pour slow: turtles paddling,
their gentle blades I could not feel.

Mary Magdalene Sings Again
Though I Did Not Touch

Who will believe this story?
He sent you back to me, our God,
to tell me not to touch you?

To tell the rest you are ascending?
What about faith?
What is this proof but torture?

They will say it was one of my dreams—
foolish woman's dreams. Witch-woman's lies,
visiting with the dead!

I thought you were the gardener called to me
at the tomb! You dared ask why I cry?
But it was your face meeting mine, the same sand at our feet.

If I had I touched you,
would you be back in our nest,
resting your clouds at my feet?

Our fragrance has not faded from our bed,
your hands rinsed from their blood.
Our children—who will care for them, O?

I could see the mountains behind you
not through you. No spirit, my guide,
my very flesh! I could have touched you.
But my hands obeyed you,
master of my hollow limbs—
shadow, or not.

You stood like my father
directing me not to touch,
me, your fallow woman.

Forgive Me That My Empirical Self Still Rules

I can cut the body of a chicken into pieces,
split its chest raw for dinner. Sever its leg.
Broil a pierced leg of lamb.

I could never be a good vegetarian.
I lost two of your babies inside me.
Three total in my life. Will not try to find more.

You left Australia to marry me.
Always a day ahead where your daughter
and parents live, your lifetime of friends, your son.

In our house
we know January
is summer and winter.

Children lean on us from both sides of the ocean.
August burns and freezes over.
An afternoon is really midnight the next day.

We are both foreigners in this country.
Yet my ex would have me ash again,
while I dine on our Phoenix.

They called you a gray fool when you came here,
yet our garden is too lush.
We have double the time, the seasons,

so many lives—
too many to display
on our shelves.

The wisdom of three marriages between
our two wedding rings,
reminding us to think of time we have left.

But I understand why Snow White's
step-mom wanted hearts locked
in their proper boxes.

I understand why ladies in Savannah,
those betrayed Southern belles, leapt
from rooftops, porches, windows to die in flight.

When you plant a
wild garden in the heat,
the roots of the Passion Flower

must
stay
cool.

Alexander Devora, Still Life Photography, San Antonio, Texas

Born in Mexico City and raised in San Antonio, Texas, Natalia Treviño was raised in Spanish by her parents while Bert and Ernie gave her English lessons on the side. Natalia is an Associate Professor of English at Northwest Vista College and a member of the Macondo Foundation, a writer's workshop aimed at encouraging non-violent social change. She graduated from UTSA's graduate English and The University of Nebraska's MFA in Creative Writing programs. Her poetry has won the Alfredo

Moral de Cisneros Award for Emerging Writers from Sandra Cisneros, the Wendy Barker Creative Writing Award, the 2008 Dorothy Sargent Rosenberg Poetry Prize, and the San Antonio Artists Foundation Literary Award. Natalia's fiction has appeared in Curbstone Press's *Mirrors Beneath the Earth* and *The Platte Valley Review*. Nonfiction essays are included in the *Wising Up* Anthologies, *Shifting Balance Sheets: Women's Stories of Naturalized Citizens* and *Complex Allegiances: Constellations of Immigration*. She is currently finishing her novel, *La Cruzada*. Often working the community programs to increase young adult literacy, she has taught classes at women's and children's shelters as well as teen detention centers. Having experienced a bi-national and bicultural life, she hopes to raise understanding between people divided by arbitrary borders. She lives with her husband, Stewart and son, Stuart just outside of San Antonio, Texas.

CPSIA information can be obtained at www.ICGtesting.com
Printed in the USA
LVOW10s0904031213

363485LV00005B/63/P